WORLD'S FAVORITE
Easy Violin Pieces

CONTENTS

TRÄUMEREI

R. SCHUMANN

MINUET AND TRIO

W. A. MOZART.

OLD VIENNESE MELODY

TRADITIONAL

THE SWAN

CAMILLE SAINT- SAËNS

MELODY IN F

ANTON RUBINSTEIN

FASCINATION

MARCHETTI
Arranged by R. Kail

rall.

rall.

THE ENTERTAINER

From *"The Sting"*

SCOTT JOPLIN
Arranged by R. Kail

(All 1st position) **Slow ragtime**

D. C. al Fine

CARNIVAL OF VENICE

TRADITIONAL

AIR for G STRING

J. S. BACH.

VALSE TRISTE

JEAN SIBELIUS

14

EVENING STAR
from "Tannhäuser"

RICHARD WAGNER
Arranged by Calvin Grooms

BARCAROLLE
from
"The Tales Of Hoffmann"

J. OFFENBACH
Arranged by Calvin Grooms

SONGS MY MOTHER TAUGHT ME

ANTON DVOŘÁK
Arranged by Calvin Grooms

BARCAROLLE

PETER ILYITCH TSCHIAKOVSKY

arr. by M. Greenwald

HUMORESQUE

ANTON DVORAK

Arranged by M. Greenwald

Poco lento e grazioso

AVE MARIA

CHARLES GOUNOD

LA BRUNETTE

EDMUND SEVERN

ADORATION

FELIX BOROWSKI

24

POEME

Zdenko Fibich

SARABANDE

J.S. Bach

Loure

INTERMEZZO
from "Cavalleria Rusticana"

GAVOTTE
from "Mignon"

A. THOMAS

SPRING SONG

FELIX MENDELSSOHN

GRAND MARCH
from "Aida"

GIUSEPPE VERDI

Tempo Marziale.

ANGEL'S SERENADE

BRAGA

VALSE
from "Mignon"

A. THOMAS

Tempo di Valse.

Fine.

KUIAWIAK

WIENIAWSKI

CRADLE SONG

HAUSER

Andantino, con molto espressione.

LEGEND

WIENIAWSKI

LIEBESGRUSS

EDWARD ELGAR

ANITRA'S DANCE

EDVARD GRIEG

*) No turn with the trills

(Piano)

REVERIE

VIEUXTEMPS

LES RAMEAUX

GUSTAVE FAURÉ

SIMPLE AVEU

F. THOMÉ

SERENATA

MOSZCOWSKI

CAVATINA

RAFF

LARGO

HÄNDEL

SPANISH DANCE

MOSZCOWSKI

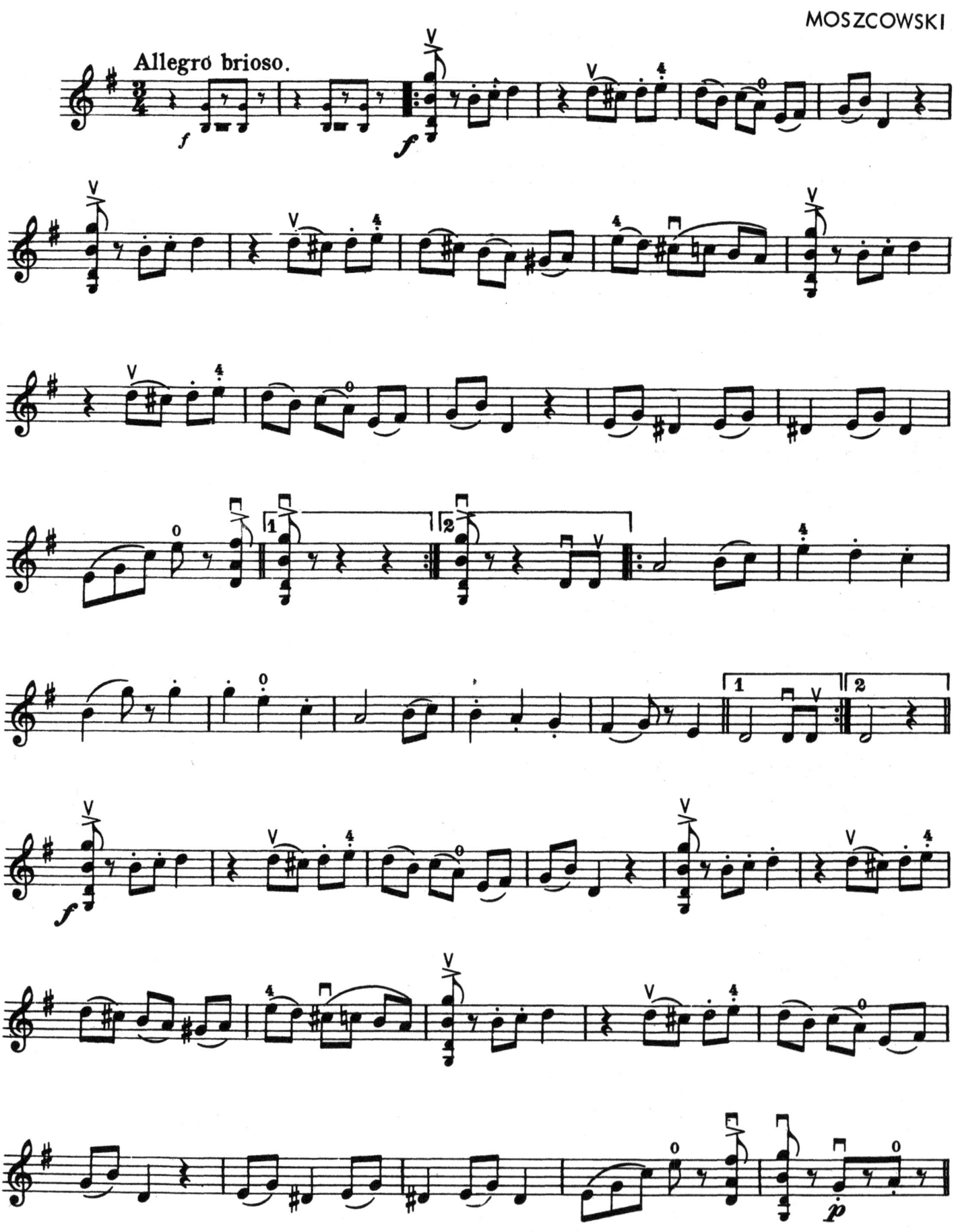